BEAST:
THE LOST CHRONICLES

Paul Stubbs born in 1969 in Norwich, is a British poet who lives between Chartres & England. He is the author of several poetry collections and books of poetical and philosophical essays. His work has appeared in various magazines and anthologies. With Blandine Longre, Stubbs has translated texts by Victor Segalen, Arthur Rimbaud, Jos Roy, and Pierre Cendors. He also co-founded the publishing house Black Herald Press in 2010. Forthcoming, *The Acceptance of Loss*, an essay on Jack Kerouac.

Also by Paul Stubbs

The Carbonized Earth, a study on Arthur Rimbaud	(Black Herald Press, 2024)
Une anatomie de l'icône / An Anatomy of the Icon	(Black Herald Press, 2022)
The Lost Songs of Gravity	(Black Herald Press, 2020)
Visions de l'Outre-monde,	(Hochroth-Paris, 2019)
The Return to Silence,	(Black Herald Press, 2016)
The End of the Trial of Man,	(Arc Publications, 2015)
Flesh,	(Black Herald Press, 2013)
Ex Nihilo,	(Black Herald Press, 2010)
The Icon Maker,	(Arc Publications, 2008)
The Theological Museum	(Flambard Press, 2005)

CONTENTS

LOST TALE FROM THE APOCRYPHA	13
THE BEAST AND THE FLOOD	14
THE BEAST AND THE GYRES	15
THE RETURN	19
THE BEAST AND THE ENIGMA OF TIME	21
GOD'S PROPHECY	23
THE BEAST AND THE COSMOLOGICAL ARGUMENT	24
DARWIN'S DOWNFALL	26
TACKLING THE CONCEPT OF TRUTH	27
THE BEAST AND THE EUCHARIST	29
COSMOLOGICAL REQUIREMENTS FOR YOUR BIRTH	31
THE VISITATION	34
THE FIRST THREE PHASES OF THE BEAST	36
THE BEAST AND THE PROBLEM OF RELIGION	39
THE END OF THE TRIAL OF MAN	41
A NEW ACCOUNT OF THE TRINITY	42
THE RELIC	44
THE APOSTATE	45
CONFRONTING THE IDEALISM V. REALISM DEBATE	46
THE ACOLYTES	47
VANITY	49
THE BEAST BEGINS LEARNING PHILOSOPHY	50
THE BEAST STUDIES THEODICY	52
THE REGENERATION	54
EXTRACTS FROM THE BEAST'S LOGBOOK	55
A DECISION	58
THE BEAST IN A STRANGE NEW CASE OF DR JEKYLL AND MR HYDE	59
THE FOREBODING	60
THE BEAST AND THE IDEA OF NOTHING	63
THE CURSE OF YEATS	65
A POSTSCRIPT TO GENESIS	67
GOD TRIES TO RESOLVE THE PROBLEM OF SIN	68
THE BEAST ESCAPES HEGEL'S SYSTEM	69
TRYING TO BECOME GOD	71

A RELIGIOUS SIDESHOW	72
THE BEAST ATTEMPTS TO BE SAVED	73
THE BEAST ENTERS HEAVEN	75
THREE POSTCARDS FROM AUSCHWITZ	76
BATTLE OF THE GODS	79
THE BEAST MEETS BISHOP BERKELEY	81
THE BEAST MEDITATES ON HIS ORIGINS	82
THE BEAST STOPS LISTENING TO MUSIC	84
THE INFAMY OF THE BEAST	85
THE NEW AWAKENING	88
THE BEAST REFUTES THE IMPORTANCE OF BARUCH SPINOZA	89
COMPLAINT	91
IDENTIFYING THE BEAST	92
THE LOOPHOLE	95
THE BEDOUIN	96
THE COSMOLOGICAL BEAST	97
EN ROUTE TO BETHLEHEM	99
SINCE THE DEATH OF YEATS	100
THE EXISTENTIAL CRISIS OF THE BEAST	104
AFTER READING KANT'S CRITIQUE OF PURE REASON	106
THE LAST STAND	108
THE BEAST PONDERS THE MOON LANDING	109
THE LAST DAYS OF THEOLOGY	111
A MATHEMATICAL FABLE	112
THE METAMORPHOSIS	114
AN ARRIVAL	115
THE INVALIDS OF ESCHATOLOGY	116
THE BEAST REFLECTS ON WHAT PART HIS ANATOMY HAS PLAYED IN CHRISTIANITY	117
SHORT SOLILOQUY OF THE POPE, BETHLEHEM	120
THE BEAST BATTLES AMNESIA	121
THE BEAST'S CRUCIFIXION	123
THE ARCHITECT	124
AFTER THE UNIVERSE	126
EPILOGUE	127
ACKNOWLEDGEMENTS	129

> ...somewhere in sands of the desert
> A shape with lion body and the head of a man,
> A gaze blank and pitiless as the sun,
> Is moving its slow thighs, while all about it
> Reel shadows of the indignant desert birds.
> The darkness drops again; but now I know
> That twenty centuries of stony sleep
> Were vexed to nightmare by a rocking cradle,
> And what rough beast, its hour come round at last,
> Slouches towards Bethlehem to be born?
>
> — W. B. Yeats, *The Second Coming*

© 2024, Paul Stubbs. All rights reserved; no part of this book may be reproduced by any means without the publisher's permission.

ISBN: 978-1-916938-64-9

The author has asserted their right to be identified as the author of this Work in accordance with the Copyright, Designs and Patents Act 1988

Cover designed by Aaron Kent

Edited and Typeset by Aaron Kent

Broken Sleep Books Ltd
PO BOX 102
Llandysul
SA44 9BG

For Blandine

PRAISE for *Beast: The Lost Chronicles*

Ever since his visionary first collection, *The Theological Mus*eum (Flambard, 2005), Stubbs has illuminated one of the most uniquely searing paths in contemporary poetry. Or perhaps it is a path away from 'contemporary poetry', invoking & travelling through worlds that often seem far from what might be considered 'contemporary poetry' in service of its orphaned recreation. To read Stubbs is to encounter prophetic relics of the future – astral bones that catch unholy in the gills – and to join a kind of anti-pilgrimage; to be but nailed down in flight, and for which the struggle towards vision becomes the visionary exploration of its own impossibility. Each poem, as each book, doubles outer and inner space to wheel its blur in the estranged flesh of resurrection.

Turning entire histories of theology and thought around his own visionary interrogation in *Beast: The Lost Chronicles*, Paul Stubbs, it will become clear to any reader, writes unlike anyone else. Always searching and questioning, conjuring a dark astronomy of flesh while summoning rot in a timeless cathedral, Stubbs incants poetry as a seer whose otherworldly sight is not of now or then but of a timeless chaos. Courageous, and darkly comic, *Beast* is a mythic, desolate, and roaming testament to what poetry, in the 21st century, might still become. Lurching between a held breath and the last gasp is the slouch of that which undoes all.
— David Spittle

In this book, Paul Stubbs has achieved something new, and wonderful. In a battle far fiercer than that of Milton's angels, the mind declares war on itself—and wins.
— Peter Oswald

In this tremendous collection, Paul Stubbs borrows Yeats' figure of the 'rough beast' (from 'The Second Coming') as a protagonist to guide us through the theological ruins of Christendom.

After two millennia, the first Christ is now a cipher: a 'hologram', 'a dust cloud', 'a ventriloquist's dummy', 'a skeleton in a space suit', a mannequin, a papier-mâché idol burning in flames. In his place the rough beast is making his passage through the lines of these poems, curious about philosophy, mathematics, music, the nature of evil, cosmology, evolution. The beast holds nothing sacred and sets about 'breaking open the cages' of our conceptual worlds.

Paul Stubbs creates a dazzling iconography and syntax with the power to evoke the theological wasteland after Nietzsche's death of God, where the horizons of truth and morality have been wiped away and we are 'straying through an infinite nothing'.

The beast—it is very clear—is beyond salvation. The question Stubbs leaves unspoken is what has and will become of us, in a cold and disenchanted universe, and without a god to save us.
— Hugh Rayment-Pickard

Beast:
The Lost Chronicles

Paul Stubbs

Broken Sleep Books

LOST TALE FROM THE APOCRYPHA

Being by Calvary's turbulence unsatisfied,
The uncontrollable mystery on the bestial floor.
— W. B. Yeats

A vile-voiced child who, kidnapped
at birth, is then carried off in secret to

    a rib-ruined town...

(*to invoke and make fly the unbiblical,*
the talon-blunted amputees in paradise)

whilst in Bethlehem, in haste, a few
hours after, the miscarriage of Mary

    is confirmed.

THE BEAST AND THE FLOOD
   The waters of religion recede and leave behind swamps and ponds
    — Nietzsche

—Noah emptying the final rusting bucket
of the flood; as, in these, these post-diluvial

days (between man and his next *named* guise),
you, the beast, arrive, impatiently pacing

the last recalcitrant deck boards of the Ark.
While God (in two minds?) he kneads

                still furiously the
                gills on your neck.

THE BEAST AND THE GYRES
*and all things run
on that unfashionable gyre again.*
— W. B. Yeats

An anthropomorphic about-turn, as gods climb free of icons,

        and you, you scowl,
        because *only* still a

man on all fours; for

only as a portent in the goggling eye of some haruspex or priest
        can you be known.
        You, sat hunched at

the womb-door of Mary, unable still to comprehend good *or* evil,
until the next generation wheels back in Christ's mannequin,

        and epistemologists in
        the pope's head build

a mind-sized matchstick model of the universe...when

        God, *before* atheism,

he fails to kill off the human virus growing inside of him,

        allowing Hitler to be born
        (sin to suppurate science).

When all Homo sapiens feel it: your beast-tail at their coccyx,
a lion's paw instead of a hand; as Buddhists atop mountains

>   abort their bodies,
>   to breathe back *your*
>
>   body into the void...

While World War II struggles now to reach a beach, and the
disembodied are impeached, as Nietzsche's soul returns,

when heaven-wasted muscle attaches once more to living bone,

>   and in a new cone we
>   hear a phone ring, as a

blackhole, it narrows into the horn of the first wax cylinder phonograph

to play *your* voice? to earplug the damned and/or force the saved
>   to raise a mirror and *deflect*
>   God's light away from them,

>   to leave their attenuated

rapt trunks to blink alone in blackness... as you, the beast,
you squeeze into the passage at Thermopylae, where even

>   worms start to mistake
>   *your* spear holes for the
>
>   five holy holes in Christ...

For like castrato singers with laryngitis, the angels in heaven
        now cannot sing, and
        all love for God it dies,

    until Dante is born and

those in the Empyrean drool, to watch collapse (again?) the gyre
        unable still to release you.

While you, anaesthetized by sin, you wait, with a hypothetical yet
        serrated grin, for all time?

until your own church, from behind the clouds emerges, and the whole of Christianity is reduced to the unexploded hand grenade of your heart,

        pinless and ready now to
        blast Christ apart, if God

    imagines *you* on the cross...

On the day when Kierkegaard and Hegel in a corridor meet, and you,
        you wake up swaddled still
        in Yeats soul, like a thermal

    foil blanket draped about you,

to keep *you* alive long enough for thought to outthink thought... and for

        one final appearance of
        Caesarism to subjugate who?

As you, through the final rusted drainpipe of a gyre you drop,
        to *stop* history repeating

      itself with your birth.

THE RETURN
For Peter Oswald

> *What if one day or night a demon came to you in your most solitary solitude and said to you: 'This life, as you now live it and have lived it, you will have to live again, and innumerable times again, and there will be nothing new in it; but rather every pain and joy, every thought and sigh, and all the unutterable trivial or great things in your life will have to happen to you again, with everything in the same series and sequence'.*
> — Nietzsche

Having only just descended a rock of pre-Christian Christs

    (nailed to burnt crosses),
    we locate you, traversing

the same linoleum bland-stretch of mnemonic sand,
rotted and rebirthed into the same unutterable body:
a time-machine with the handbrake on... or urn-emptying

    lump of land-blubber,

for like a god caught lagging upon a stairwell between
heaven and hell, you'll try *anything* to sidestep culpability,

    like holding your breath
    until the universe passes,

or by sandblasting all fossils, to self-adjust your descendants
    and place yourself in the
    wrong historical time-zone...

before then pickling your organs, your intestines and brain,
    (for all future generations?)

       until humankind is ill again,
       bedridden by *your* lapsed guilt

(to leave you holding a compass, a map and an unrustable sextant,
but still unable to get back to that pyramidal rock of Nietzsche...)

       Thus, not until memory,
       a fountainhead, has run

dry of human days, and you, the beast, in your 2000th year?
       wake to your own now
       rib-retractable progeny,

can *amor fati* be reversible, and the cycle

       of theology complete.

THE BEAST AND THE ENIGMA OF TIME
Immobility is but a picture (in the photographic sense of the word) taken of reality by our mind.
— Henri Bergson

Unable still to accept that your time spent on earth
    could be recorded by clocks, or that
        (one day) any future point in theology

        could catch up with you...

you, you abandon it, what? the continuity
    between what's born and what's dead,

before deciding (instead?)
    to simply peer over and beyond the balls
        of your own eyes to witness it: consciousness

    float free finally of the universe...

refusing (as you do) to allow mobility, immobility, or in fact any form
        of kinetics to define you.

But why? well, to enable you to rip up measurable time
like concrete
    from the always shifting fixture of space...

        to leave not any
            geometrical trace of strata
                beneath your body weight,

to leave you paralyzed, and gaping at it: the *annihilation of the real*,

>   like water glittering infinitely
> in front of you,
>   across which skim souls like
>   stones thrown by exultant gods...

As you, in order to escape finally the fallacy of segmented time,
you chew through your own bowels to reach it: pure *durée*... to start

>   the collapse of homogeneity.

Until only one event can unnail you from the cross of spatiality:
the determinist locating a single free aspect of your *slouch*,

>   that, or the past-present-future
>   structure of time, in all minds,
being (simultaneously) revoked when you, at last, reach it:
Bethlehem...

there, where no quantitatively comparable time
>   with any other in the universe will help scientists
>   predict now the trajectory

>   of your path.

GOD'S PROPHECY
its hour come round at last
— W. B. Yeats

When your udders begin leaking Christian blood, you'll hear it,
from the bottom of a staircase, before a door in hell's basement:
> *'You will be born'*

Throughout a lipless land of switched-off microphones,
into which the disinherited scream out in vain God's name:
> *'You will be born'*

As the last person to see you dissolves on your tongue,
and your mouth eats off your own ear until hearing it:
> *'You will be born'*

Before a sudden involuntary stampede, as the saved, running off
the leg-braces of their human bones, they overtake you, singing:
> *'You will be born'*

Until the day when the love-lapsed you has been pushed through into
a world of no-bone, cartilage, or sinew, and you finally understand what
> *'You will be born'* means...

having fed for centuries on geckos, gnats, and dead scorpions
to sustain that still unborn second Christ in your diaphragm,

> until you in your
> real body were born.

THE BEAST AND THE COSMOLOGICAL ARGUMENT

Desperate to refute Aquinas' notion
    that every object that moves must have *first*
        been moved by something else,

you, you try resting, an incalculable theorem,

    between the potentiality
    of moving and the actuality
    of ever doing so...

before then hurrying to obliterate the entire Argument

    by pulling a light cord to switch
    off the universe in God's head.

But why? and to what end? well, in order to confirm
    (to yourself)

that the death of cosmology would *not* (you decide)

    create a vacuum in substance,
    but only in fact an uncaused
    (animalized?) mutation of it.

So, seeing that you, not God, are now the greatest
    thought any living extant thing can *think*,
        you decide to prove it, by going further

and annihilating substance forever...

yes, but how?

by both devouring and then regurgitating your own carcass

>   (to reinstate God's ubiquity
>   immediately as merely a half-
>   digestible substitute for matter...)

so that nothing whatsoever in the starless spaces around
you now can move, or stop, or even begin existing again,

>   until you, finally, you finish
>   eating it, the last remaining

page of the *Summa Theologiae* as, in Bethlehem,

owing to the (still?) non-traceable contingency
>   of your birth, the Five Ways of proving God's existence
>   >   are, by you, reduced
>   >   to NONE...

DARWIN'S DOWNFALL
> *It is not the strongest of the species that survives, nor the most intelligent that survives. It is the one that is the most adaptable.*
> — Charles Darwin

When scrubbing the fossils of mammals, reptiles
and amphibians, but finding not one distinguishing

characteristic of any single genus that can be traced
back to *you*...thus, in despair, at night, on the Beagle,

>we hear him, Darwin, hollering:
>*'Get off of this island, Beast!'*

>realizing the goal of genealogy
>by you had already been reached.

TACKLING THE CONCEPT OF TRUTH
What is the concept of truth as correspondence with reality for?
— Leszek Kołakowski

        In defiance against the supposition that
        what, in truth, *must* be considered true,
you, the beast,

begin by breaking open the cages of concepts,
        to free them: the answers,
        held hostage by mankind...

        until the world-tinted spectacles
        of existence from your eyeballs
are lifted, and you finally see?

yes, until so bamboozled by *real* reality, you clamber

        up suddenly onto the high, heavenly

        and giddying terraces of God's skull,

if only to see (for the first time) his pure unmediated vistas of truth...

        forcing you to substitute
yourself for any artificial reconstruction of it,
        reality....

        and, in order to stop worshipping
            only
        illusion, misconception, falsity?

you begin doing this:

set humanity a series of unsolvable problems that not one genius on earth

        could fathom...

        but how? well,

    by sand-erasing the contrast between *less* and *more*, *order* and *disorder*, *being* and *non-being*

        until not even God can prove
        whether he is contingent or not...

Thus now we witness you, the beast, from this day on, head
    down and frantic to finish them: your mathematically
        impossible proofs

        that will one day
        refute the world.

THE BEAST AND THE EUCHARIST
For Alice Oswald

Hatred of God may bring the soul to God
— W. B. Yeats

    Today, in church, at the
    Eucharist, you, ready to
bowdlerize theodicy and start your stopwatch
    on all human sin, whilst
demoting him, the priest, to a ventriloquist
    dummy on *your* knee...

As you, wanting to replace every
    genetic-proof body of a deity with
yourself, you start planning for it:
    the rebooting of God... yes, but how
exactly?

    by ripping off his VR headsets
    from the pupilless white eyes
of the saved in heaven...

and by reconstructing the resurrection
    using electric charge, a voltmeter, even a handle
to shock Christ's soul back suddenly
    into the *wrong* corpse...

for to postpone Christianity? you would (you decide)

need first to garrotte Adam, then every
    subsequent figure in Bethlehem, to leave
        three incongruous crosses on a hill...

    which would then confirm that
only *one* of the following must (ecclesiastically?) be decided upon:
    Christ a) always existed in God,
    b) did not always exist in God,
    or, *and maybe, to you, even more likely*, c) only
existed in you?

Thus now, feeling at last teleologically clear about
    who should be substituted
        for whom, and *when*, you,
            you depart, with each

now not-quite biblical anatomy pushing past you to sin...

    —As you, finally, you experience it:
        theophany, Christ-clone
        your mannequin within.

COSMOLOGICAL REQUIREMENTS FOR YOUR BIRTH
When a vast image out of Spiritus Mundi
Troubles my sight
— W. B. Yeats

First, heaven to be frittered down to a place of skulls...
        then theology, suddenly,
        to the sundial, to return,

when Christ's deep space skeleton re-enter's earth's atmosphere,

        and apes in their cages
        begin to cross themselves.
Before astronauts, they take off their spacesuits, and breathe...
        as space-time collapses,

        and the end of religion over
        loudspeakers is announced,

forcing the pope, upon his cardinals, to perform the Heimlich manoeuvre,

        to remove God's lodged
        word from their throats...

until faith to its planet of origin returns, and the four horsemen, dejected,
        they trot back into a barn.

        As the three persons of the
        trinity (until you're born)
        they are *forced* to hold up
in front of their face Yeats' face mask upon a stick,

until God's own subcutaneous udders begin then

>> to secrete (by accident?)
>> man's now unusable blood...

>> as, in a far-away corner of
>> the universe, upon an asteroid,
>> a signpost with the word 'God'
>> written on it begins to fade...

stretching the then unused celestial skin of the saved across your
>> crass and attenuated trunk

(*like a straitjacket placed there by the last person to ever sin*)

>> which will begin then
>> *theologically* to fit. And
>> thus this will

>> (ultimately?) constitute it:

your first recalcitrant attempt to be born, your first frigid attempt
>> to exhale it: Christ's *last*
>> breath, to thus bring forth

a body the bible never promised us, into Bethlehem...

there, where the final priest, in expectation of your arrival, he will
>> have started already to fix
>> up his noose, wire-bind his
>> own hands behind his back,

and who will not, no matter what happens next, pray for

    anyone to unfasten him.

THE VISITATION
> *A crowd*
> *Will gather, and not know it walks the very streets*
> *Whereon a thing once walked that seemed a burning cloud*
> — W. B. Yeats

For an interloper like you meant never to exist?
only so many bogus sightings in the wilderness,

>> only so many walking-
>> frames, leg-braces and

orthopaedic sticks left littering the desert
> by the last men to
> attempt your gait...

Thus, each century, (by mistake?) you eye-gouge
> the members of all
> still hooded clergies:

(*to leave each priest yammering, faith-stricken and petrified*
> *to be banging a gong*)

>> as, onto the unbiblical
>> soul-scape of all those

still scripted to see you, you, against *their* will?
rear up: a dust-cloud or hologram in place of the
> theophany of Christ,

to leave you, here, (today?) in this world of theodicy
and coterminous plight, as *only* an aping, of the
> soteriological hope

in man that cannot
now deliver a thing... whatever

the outcome of sin.

THE FIRST THREE PHASES OF THE BEAST
And yet, twice born, twice buried, grow he must,
Before the full moon, helpless as a worm
  — W. B. Yeats

NEW MOON

Not quite an anthropological anomaly, or sin-free
        foetus attempting in vain
        to hold it: Christ's breath,

and with only a still lignified sense of immortality
forcing the first three trunks of theology to gasp, gasp
        because unable still
        to utter your name,

        as, from behind your brain,

the known biblical universe it lifts up its curtain
        to reveal the ventriloquial

        dummy of God mouthing
        your first human words,

as, the auxiliary bone-gears of your lower spine, they begin now
        suddenly to select it: a gait
        to withstand a second cross...

Waxing Crescent

Only the vaguest sense of a religious purpose
urging you suddenly to suck on and inhale

>   a canister full of
>   Adam's last breath,

when you, biologically determined to *never* sin,
you claw back the bark from the trees in Eden

>   to reveal *your* bone.

The correct biblical decibel level of your howl
>   unable to be reached...

until in desperation, you exhume them: the jawbones
>   of all who cried out
>   to Christ on the cross.

as you, (as if thrust up unexpectedly through
>   a trapdoor in sand)

>   you look up to hear:

the horror of the hammering of the tent pegs,
>   of the first faith-rushed
>   canopy of your church.

FIRST QUARTER

Your soul-filament flickering, a theophanic pang,
and a blindfolded, still post-theological tribe

>> sat speechless in front
>> of a glass of *your* blood

(*speechless until a spacesuit, containing Christ's
own bones, has floated free of epistemology...*)

as you, amid the last death-struggles in theology,
>> you curl up into a ball at
>> God's feet, into a zero,

to take part in it: the incalculable arithmetic of sin,
by subtracting *yourself* from the following:
>> bibles, horns, hearts,

from even Job's own unsalvageable body-parts... as every
last equation results in *you*: the rib-spitting doppelgänger
>> of a messiah unborn,
>> *unborn* until soteriology

it makes of your body an impasse and (for every
spiritually insolvent race in retreat?) a last faithless

>> dispensation against
>> eternity, and defeat...

THE BEAST AND THE PROBLEM OF RELIGION

> *That twenty centuries of stony sleep*
> *Were vexed to nightmare by a rocking cradle*
>   — W. B. Yeats

    On this blue oval that bears no relation
    to your kind, in which you decided to
reset the auxiliary gears of your spine to sidestep heaven, and
        not wait
        like man, a trapped fly,
for the god-spider, in the web at the centre of our
        galaxy
(and having only just out-leaped Christ in the Ascension
        using a
        jet pack...)

we find you wrapped up and huddled
        in faith-repellent hides,
to protect your own body *from* religion,
        until on the day when
your own acolytes arrive: Bedouins, hierophants, cabalists,
        playing drums, tubas,
while listening to your howl, windily recorded, on an old
        phonograph in the sand.

(Scientists suddenly blackboard-wiping
        all equations that
will not result in *you*, that cannot decipher *your*
        biological untruth).

    You, short-circuiting
all celestial grids with your presence, before
        watching it, the atom

turn into a tear upon Christ's cheek,
while envisioning a rank future orthodoxy of beast
        worshipping beast...

but a reason then at least for you to start proselytizing men? Yes,
        but only after hypnotizing
        Adam out of his own sin,
and by imagining it his face, in transit, between blank
        biblical stares, as you,
from God's skull, you tweezer free the Word,
        until a new bible opens...
and we find them your own ribless offspring
        huddling in close to see:
        (in place of the Magi?)
        you, swaddled in Christ's clothes,

        and desperate for someone to teach.

THE END OF THE TRIAL OF MAN
Man is a beast of prey.
— Oswald Spengler

Upon the floorboards of the final church, amid the
blood and the death-throes of gods, the rough beast
has eaten its last, has eaten and spat out man's rib;

                eaten and spat and stamped
down its feet onto the now crushed and unrecognizable
                     death mask of Yeats:

                     one mile outside
                     of Bethlehem...

A NEW ACCOUNT OF THE TRINITY
We all speak of it, though we may not speak of it as it truly is.
— St Augustine

—When the trinity appeared, sobbing, in despair,
and bickering between its three parts due to their

    incompatibility,

it decided to scuttle off in search of an addendum,
    a missing, still
      elusive fourth part...

searching high and low for whatever from nothingness

    could be salvaged
    and added to itself.

So that instead of living out time sat perched on
its own soul's buttresses and heavenly summits

    to attain the highest
    holy vantage-point

from which to survey its internal vistas alone, it decided

(in seven days?) to create the universe to help recover it:

    this missing, still
    elusive fourth part...

Until, on the eighth day, in despondency, when
all three parts arrived in person to plead with him,

the beast, to 'join up please and make us feel whole!'

it left him, finally, with no other choice but to re-scatter it:
    the trinity,

    by dragging
    back God's soul into the wilderness.

THE RELIC
> *What have we to do*
> *But stand with empty hands and palms turned upwards*
> *in an age which advances progressively backwards?*
> — T. S. Eliot

Upon this day, fresh from a god's crypt
or catacomb, you, the beast (a blunt and

impractical end to Historical theology), arrive,
        struggling to surmise
        just what it is, this relic,

this contraption fallen into desuetude,
        half-buried in sand,

where every hour, in every century, blindfolded
        and tonsured beings
        (in case of *your* birth)

keep attempting to repair it: a prayer-machine...

        (invented, built, then
        abandoned by aliens?)

the only still extant piece of machinery
in the universe designed to re-open them:
        Christ's wounds...

        re-open them to stop man
        copulating with beasts.

THE APOSTATE

It is the time of the gods who have fled and of the god who is coming.
— *Martin Heidegger*

At Mass, today, we run-in to him, the beast,
struggling to confront Christ's skeleton there,

struggling to sit out God's decomposition in the
        pope's chair...

CONFRONTING THE IDEALISM V. REALISM DEBATE
For David Spittle

By holding your breath, and only *pretending*
to die, forcing all matter to cease to exist...

      allowing you, the beast, to become
      (temporarily?) an idealist—

So that when the realist appears brandishing
his mind-sized mould cast of the nothingness
abandoned by Kant outside of time and space

you, unwilling to be positioned in *any* place,
(whether calculable or incalculable)
      you simply stall,

      stall and refuse

outright to *only* symbolically exist, or even subsist,
      until the alarm

clock (set by Bergson) it begins to *intuitively* ring,

      to wake you suddenly
      beyond the noumenal...

there, where (for all eternity?) truth itself begins:
with a noose, a ladder, and God's last oxygen canister,
      on your first day

      outside the skull.

THE ACOLYTES
The corpses of numberless generations of men lie heaped in your dust
— Rabindranath Tagore

From whose government or secret papal
       files did a first fake
       photo of you emerge?

For even the clergy in Rome glimpse your face

       in every single pew.

You, shouting down religion with a megaphone
every time flesh (your own) is stretched back

across man's skull, to re-imagine him: as a disguised

       (mistaken?) inhabitant
       of your own soul...

(*to guarantee that nothing but your own surfeited body*
       is eaten in all feasts)

For the sweat on you is the sweat on priests,
the result of two thousand years of allegiance

       to a judicial rule

requiring only that each MP, judge, or terrorist
drops on all fours, dons a lion-mask, and howls...

until even tattooed tribesmen start to idolize
>	you; those who,

in lieu of Christ, left their forest simply to cull,
cook or crucify any man who didn't believe in you:

those still (today?) searching for you in folktales,

>	in old bibles,
>	or on papyrus

and, perhaps less believable, on maps unfolded
by the esoteric; so that, each week, the initiated

can meet to discuss how you've blindsided them
>	into theosophy,

black magic, medievalism, Rosicrucianism too?
the same members of a secret society who will
(millennially?) drink your acidic blood to excess,

to *keep* God dead? Yes, and to make sure poachers

>	go on hunting
>	you, in Africa.

VANITY

Half-hoarsely mouthing: '*Eloi, Eloi, lama sabachtani!*'
you lurch with no memory across the hot desert floor.

>A sin-suspended beast like you
>need remember nothing more.

THE BEAST BEGINS LEARNING PHILOSOPHY

Today, pondering Zeno, we encounter you,
role-playing the tortoise to Christ's Achilles,
and winning the race by holding a starting
               pistol to God's head,
                   to *beat* eternity to the line,

               and slow souls suddenly
               to a soteriological sludge...

until, tomorrow? when fire-hosing Plato's cave,
and stamping out the final flame of 'appearance'

               (to lunge past the rubble
               of reality and really *see)*

you, studying the problems of philosophy, *just* to become
the fly in the 'fly bottle' in Wittgenstein's head, the head
of animals, insects, birds too; while (laughingly) doubting

               if, in fact, any problem
               could be free of you!

lolling dead centre as you do in the chalk circle
of man's consciousness, incapable of escaping
until you, you find a way in which to swallow the

               empirical world *whole*.

Thus, EVERYDAY (if only to confirm Hume's theory about
the presumption of probability taken from experience?), you *slouch*...

> while feasting on titbits of *Dasein*
> out of Heidegger's own palm
>
> (fed through the zoological
> bars of the ribcage of every
> philosopher you've killed),

you, an antinomy because unable still to find a philosopher
capable of untangling it, *your* truth; until when you, finally,

in your final lesson, you decide that there is no epistemologist

> (not even Kant) who might,
> potentially, release you from that
> thought-caul in Yeats' head.

Thus, you conclude that not *one* philosopher in the world is for you,
and that, instead of cultivating a way to read them sincerely,
> you'll do this: *eat* their books,
> dismiss every hubristic theory,

until on the day when leaving class, you megaphone
your own philosophical category, a new notion on how to
keep men away from both God *and* Bethlehem: (which you call)

> *The Validity of Self-improvement
> through Sin.*

THE BEAST STUDIES THEODICY

Today, enrapt at the trial of Eichmann,
we watch you, as you study it, theodicy,

taking down notes and wanting (above all) to *try* it:
        genocide, rape, incest,
           maybe even necrophilia...

until the mass suffering of the Jew *stops*, Satan,
        on his sunbed, *yelps*,
        and (inside your head)

all of history's worst crimes: the holocaust, atomic bomb,
        patricide, and mass
        public hangings are

turned *back* into folktales, children's stories, comedies
to be planted at birth by God into each new baby's head.

But what then when even death no longer interests you? you gorge
        instead on God's word,

           attempting *omnipotently*
           to decode it, muttering:

'Evil *cannot* be in accordance with the ubiquitous causal
activities of a creator, fideism, natural laws, or original sin!'

As then so pumped up, *why*-clogged, and raging,
you imagine hanging, drawing, and quartering them:

>   Leibniz, Arnauld,
>   Malebranche, etc.

(to begin the final rational breakdown of mankind to its
>   last molecule of sin).

Until when finally, in a graveyard, in Bethlehem? we relocate you
>   reading the decalogue...

there, where, (for the duration of whim) *your* mockery
of the Sixth Commandment '*Thou shalt not kill*' begins,
>   with you muttering
>   'Why? Why? Why?'

>   knowing that no
>   laws to you apply.

THE REGENERATION
I should be glad of another death
— T. S. Eliot

—A now rapacious primate, the beast, driving
the Taoist, the Christian, the Hindu and
the Muslim back onto all fours, and forcing

      a new plague of people
to re-remove
      and display case the rib...

(*without* gods the world, re-judging the pelvis,
unwraps the linen of Christ from a lion's bones)

—Until when at least a hundred evolutionary
mutations up ahead, and a billion cold years along...
(*onto an eschatological and lunar terrain*)

You, the beast,
      you'll rise up again, freed

finally of the
      microbiology of religions, and

           coterminous continents of sin.

EXTRACTS FROM *THE BEAST'S LOGBOOK*

> *These are the only legible pages recovered from the logbook consisting of theological musings, random observations, fragments of ideas for big homiletic speeches, prophetic scribblings, personal anecdotes. While the pages salvaged are undated, experts (who, for the sake of coherence, have numbered these extracts) believe them to have been written sometime during the last two thousand years.*

1) First light, trees like turbines. Unrelenting assault by sand, and much too far to go. Every day the same teleological need to commit an act of terrible violence on priests.

2) Noticeable increase in body fat. One rib partly broken. All night the sound of angels passing close by in the darkness like large military trucks. Goose pimples all over my body informing me theology is over. Scabs suddenly falling like loose rooftiles from my wounds.

3) Sin-addled, I awake at dusk, thinking the next civilization may not be born in a womb, thinking am I the race-retractable god who will arise after God dies? Am I the true meaning of the Word after the abyss has gone? In the end am I the beginning?

4) A vision, constant, of Rome on fire: distant smouldering churches, ruined gothic arches, St Peter's basilica in flames, and thousands upon thousands of naked zombies tearing off the last bloody shreds of a priest's chasuble. Most structures destroyed.

5) In the middle of the plain, pregnant women kneeling and screaming out my name. Beside jar after jar of pickled wombs, men engraving tablets. To think clearly now seems impossible. As, at my side, an army of Hyenas gather, moving in droll, half-heretical movements. While above me an eagle flying low hovers, unable to eat carrion or land.

6) Too many visions, multiple tunnels and wormholes twisting into outer space that refuse to admit me. All kinds of dream-episodes of myself and Christ conversing on the cross. Lightening stealing the spine from my body and then returning it. Mourning and lament, laughter, mine. Something *other* than myself wanting to take possession of my soul.

7) Church bells ringing. Members of an unknown religious order wearing sandwich-boards protest my existence. Soundless large falcons failing to land on my shoulder. Biblically dark clouds building in the west. Skeletons abandoned to catafalques on the horizon. Bloody shrouds flapping.

8) A vow: On the day when I re-find Yeats fussing about in a cave or in his study, taking down notes, and worrying about the end of the world, I'll end this.

9) Heavy-lidded with too much pre-world sleep. Too many thoughts come to nothing. Come to this: axioms that bleed, scabious rage, and an inclination to hide, always to hide, to crawl back, temporarily infinitized, under the carapace of my human skull.

10) In honour of ME: let us have a one-minute silence in public squares, in offices and on football pitches to commemorate those (already) worm-eaten parts of me that decay, every day, I fail either to reach Ben Bulben *or* Bethlehem.

11) This morning... drinking the blood of men not holy enough to resist me. Using the eye-sockets of their skulls as if binoculars, seeing a mirage of myself, on the horizon, eating God. What omen is this? What hour arrives?

12) Various figures, hooded, chanting incoherently in a line beside me. (Some of them praying, some of them not). One or two of them running up ahead of me, holding maps, sextants, setting up theodolites in the sand, and grinning. Mirages?

13) Half-buried in the sand up ahead of me, an altar of incense, smoking. A blindman feeling for my soul in braille. His fingers bleeding. Two of the trinity bandaged and limping and refusing to meet my stare. Flies, in broken ranks, failing theologically to negotiate my shape.

14) Is that city coming closer? Am I the only survivor of the final religious war? I seem to be killing everything, that or performing a strange dance like that atheist yesterday dragging in circles the steel-trap I set for him. I NEED bandages, medicine, anything to dull the pain of being a lapsed Christ. There is no point then in NOT asking it... am I human?

15) Irreparable muscle-damage in my lower back. Progress almost impossible. Body too heavy to push, like dragging an ancient entablature through sand. Both of my eyes are bloodshot, my half-human face half-erased. Reality also becoming dangerously displaced.

16) Last note to myself: refrain from roaming alone at night in open spaces, graveyards, auditoriums, churches... remain inside, turn off the lights, DON'T read the bible. Stay alive.

A DECISION
Things thought too long can be no longer thought
— W. B. Yeats

It no longer seems necessary for you to reach Bethlehem,
or to even need still to drag Yeats' foetus out of a gyre

    on your arrival there:

your dream of garrotting Nietzsche instead of Christ
upon the cross has already unbalanced you enough to

    have your own unborn body
    cryogenically preserved in a lab:

    in case of eternal recurrence.

THE BEAST IN A STRANGE NEW CASE OF DR JEKYLL AND MR HYDE

Today, in a priest's chair, in St Peter's Square,
we locate you, half-asleep, and delirious still

>   in your half-
>   torn chasuble...

delirious still, but beginning now finally to
wake from it: your own (worst?) nightmare that

>   religion's real...

THE FOREBODING
The best lack all conviction, while the worst
Are full of passionate intensity
— W. B. Yeats

When the holiest man
unexpectedly *irritated*
by holiness on top of a mountain
(in a sudden splash of metaphysical oils, theological syrups,
and celestial goo...) he
feels you, the beast, burst forth out of
the porthole of his soul.

While in graveyards, villages,
jungles all over the world, papier-mâché
idols of Christ are (involuntarily?)
set on fire, as the still-beating hearts of
atheists, by you? are torn out,
torn out and piled steaming
at the foot of caryatids on an entablature
of a first church found on
Mars...

Until on all altars, in all galaxies,
in all banquets left by the
spiritually famished, *your* rank carcass is devoured.
Devoured and turned into trinkets,
into new fake signs of the zodiac or ugly
paganistic charms,

as the saved desperate to leave our planet queue
up now at the door of a spaceship behind trees...

while not one person in the universe seems now
        capable of being born twice
(being too womb-suspended to break the spell
        of another pre-planetary sleep).
So that only cultists, soothsayers, and hierophants
        appear now capable of mistaking
        your body for their own...

causing a Hindu, Islamist, Buddhist also
        to solemnly unveil, unrobe...
because of a cataleptic foreboding of *you*? Yes,
and because of the god-eating grumble of
        your syncretic digestion overground,
that, and by what, if anything, might be
        left of you in the memory

        of all those still following
        Osiris, Vishnu, Allah, etc.
        As angel's finally miscarry Christ's foetus
and, towards a tumulus inscribed
        with Yeats' last words on your whereabouts:
        patriarchs, in rags, they
        begin *en masse* to march...

        Until only in Bethlehem can
residents still be found at night romping in
        wolf's skins in search of you,
        the sin-recyclable generations
who will *not* tell their children what nightmares of you,
        the beast, might (theologically?)

        allude to, or why rhapsodic,
        yet at the same time *horripilated*
        by their visions of your
        never-to-be actualized birth,
they themselves

        cannot stop still praying for it.

THE BEAST AND THE IDEA OF NOTHING
> *Now, if we could prove that the idea of the nought, in the sense in which we take it when we oppose it to that of existence, is a pseudo-idea, the problems that are raised around it would become pseudo-problems.*
> — Henri Bergson

You, today, refusing to become nothing,

forcing Berkeley (via the Heimlich manoeuvre)
      to spit out his idea of you,

you exist
      wrinkling and unwrinkling:
      a hiatus in the resurrection,

you exist
      finding a print of *your* face
      hidden on the Turin shroud,

you exist
      even when substituted
      for the thing-in-itself,

you exist
      managing to disembowel God
      (only your own guts spill out)

you exist

looking and then not looking at the world,
      (annihilating external objects
      in-between, except yourself)

you exist
      (with your own spinal-column
      unexpectedly now a crowbar
      to lever space and time apart,

enough for yourself or Einstein or Kant to squeeze through).

As, at the end of the final millennia
        we locate you: the last *beep*
        heard on the heart monitor
        of God before he flatlines...
        and with only a hologram of Christ
        left flickering in deep space
        (and with no real epistemological
way left now of perceiving anything).

        Until, when stepping free finally
        of the never-to-be actualized
        ash-heaps of nothingness, zero,
        zilch, fuck all...
        wearing only Bergson's small
        moustache to make you visible,
we see you.

THE CURSE OF YEATS
I call it death-in-life and life-in-death
— W. B. Yeats

You, the Beast, in Dublin, feasting on an upturned garbage
        can and reading *The Tower*
        under a streetlight for a clue,

you, chewing on the word-carrion, the ground down pulp of
the Irish lexicon: using your large rotatable jaws to destroy it, while
        dreaming of a new tongue,
        palate, and upper diaphragm

that will allow you to speak directly to God, and *only* God
        (without Berkeley blasting
        your atoms into shrapnel?)

you, grimacing and straining to attain your most Yeatsian face,
        as your veins coagulate with
        the unused ink from *his* pen...

But no, you do not believe in parallelism, and you have never
yet met Yeats *or* God. And thus, in public, you are forced to remain it:
        a daguerreotype of a dog
        eating on a priest's doorstep

(to resume the age-old allegorical cycle of you growing fat
        and stodgy on human sin).

Until when, each night, in a room above the alleyway in which you sleep,
        a light in a study comes on,
        Yeats' book is taken down

and you, you are forced (again?) to heave past yourself, to lean

>   biblically into it, the agony
>   of your Eden-uprooting cry...

(before convulsing and juddering and upchucking on all fours)
because unable right *there* in the street to miscarry him, Yeats,

>   until the miscarriage of mankind.

A POSTSCRIPT TO GENESIS
How lovely the world must have been
Before the arrival of man
— Giuseppe Ungaretti

On the eve of the very first day of creation
only nothingness stirs (nothing else could)

until you, the beast, the *first* eye, you lift up
the curtains of your eyelids to allow the world

>>to be staged,
>>and to feel the

still inconstant floorboards of insufficient reality
creak beneath the weight of extended sudden matter...

(while a still canvas-covered, but never-to-be finished
>>bust of God, into
>>*all* finite minds, on
>>ropes, is lowered.)

As you, gagging because unable still to regurgitate
>>truth's first codex,
you raise up a conqueror's paw to demand:

>>'Let there be man!'

>>and thus, there were men...

moving prodigiously, but mechanically, like spastic patients
>>(reaching for non-
>>negotiable handrails)

>>across uneven terrain.

GOD TRIES TO RESOLVE THE PROBLEM OF SIN
God does not so much decree sins as admit to existence certain possible substances, already involving in their complete notion, under the aspect of possibility, a free sin, and so involving the whole series of things which they will be in
— Leibniz

By tinkering with Adam, Eve, Job, and Judas
until they *feel* guilty, and then by abdicating responsibility
                for the morality
                of all of them,

before deciding (amid his first theodicean silence
on what *mea culpa* for man might ultimately mean)

to give you, the beast (at least) a *bit part* in man's
still untold story of sin: but only when managing
                (in Bethlehem?)

to wean his own still unsaved offspring off evil,

                by sucking on the nipples
                on your underside.

THE BEAST ESCAPES HEGEL'S SYSTEM
how can there be anything beyond knowledge, that is beyond mind or Geist, for Geist turns out ultimately to be identical with the whole of reality?
— Charles Taylor

On the day when consciousness, God's film
is torn from its spool by you and you finally *see*,

> to lurch then irrationally
> away from it, *idealism*...

that which had been (forever?) pestering you
to unknowingly ghost above the surface of it:

> the dead sandless desert
> of a conceptualized plain,

impatient and ready (as you always had been?)
every century, to withdraw from it: history...

like a piece of finite flotsam from the ebbing

> deterministic tides
> of absolute thought.

Until brought back to the stink, the corpse-dust,

and the post-Adamite felicity of hereditary sin,

until able, finally! to begin to subjectively die...

to be historically free, and, for the first time,
what Hegel believed no mammal, amphibian, planet or

Homo sapiens could ever be:

an *unresolvable* anomaly,

a body in search of a birth.

TRYING TO BECOME GOD

Only a few seconds after the Big Bang, we see you,

        crouched blank-brained
        on a first spat-out crag,

frustratingly fiddling with a tangle of God's own
pre-creational cables, minute optical fibres and still

        unused electrical wires;

impatient (in lieu of life?) to construct it: the switch

        that will turn on the first

        light-filaments of stars...

A RELIGIOUS SIDESHOW
> *Once out of nature I shall never take*
> *my bodily form from any natural thing*
> — W. B. Yeats

—*Between* theophanies, we locate you, the beast,

unmasked, re-robed, wearing whose torn chasuble?
        (*Partying harder than*

an atheist in the final crossless cathedral of a star)

      while catwalking the attire

of a Hinduist, a Buddhist, a Cathar? even of a priest,

as you, the beast, you cackle between the trying
        on of each new vestment:
        maniple, cassock, zucchetto...

(*while trying on and taking off gloves of human flesh*)

      until when feeling so bereft
      of all future religious dread?

you begin now tiptoeing half-naked through

      each still boarded-up
      church in God's head.

THE BEAST ATTEMPTS TO BE SAVED

(Temporarily?) on this the
most unsoteriological of days,
we encounter you, the beast, trying on and taking off
the flesh-gloves of the first
Homo sapiens ever to pray...

(While swotting up on morphology, eschatology,
taxidermy, and/or a series of the
most rudimentary books on faith)

you, training *religiously*
(taking one less breath each day)
until your torso, as thin as a wafer,
and weighing less even than
a feather on an angel's wing,

it starts randomly falling off things:
skyscrapers, citadel walls, cliff-edges etc.
to learn the choreography of a butterfly
and feign the muscle-free in heaven!

—Until God, descending to sit upon a mountain,
he starts quickly scribbling down notes, asking:

'Any underlying symptoms of redemption to note?
No...
Any neighbourly compassion for his fellow beasts?
No...

Growth of a second tongue and/or mental imbalance?
No...
Any significant new damage to his heart tissue caused
by love?
No...nothing
only the six-inch retractable bones now jutting out
from each paw where Christ's nails could have been.'

    —To leave you, the beast, unsaved and
    dead to the Vatican, mankind, whim...

and thinking: 'Only the one theodicean lapse
    in time born out of Christ's own indecision
        upon the cross could have given
            birth to an aberration like me!'

    the last soul left in theology
    unable to be undone by sin.

THE BEAST ENTERS HEAVEN

Amid unopenable bibles, blank telegrams and
the shipwrecked pelvis of God, we locate you,
tattooing the word 'Beast' onto Mary's thigh,

                elated finally to have
                replaced Christ's face.

THREE POSTCARDS FROM AUSCHWITZ

who would not fear
when God's eyes shut
and all the angels fall flat
and every creature darkens
  — Janos Pilinszky

1.
Deep in the dark of a gas chamber, shower room
(or still-to-be emptied coliseum in Hitler's head?)

>   arrive a cortège of
>   cartilaginous creatures,

headed by *you* here hooded and shouldering the
>   still unimaginable

>   coffin-size needed
>   to bury him, God…

to force Mengele (mistakenly?) into jumpstarting you
into a prophecy of man's last day on earth,

>   where wet sponged and
>   relaxed in an electric chair

we find you, nonplussed but ready to assimilate it:
>   the history of human evil
>   through your chest-straps.

2.

The half-Hitlerian heft of your body,
moving eschatologically towards us,

> or moving half-
> bandaged away?

On the day when faith it is reduced to a
slow degenerative disease of the spine

(and praying hands, they are reduced to stubs,
bloodied bandaged mementos of God's love)

> as *your* umbilical it
> tightens around the

throats of each member of the Aryan race not
now able to remember who Jesus Christ was,

> on leaving church...

3.
Two now ex-members of the human race,
stood smoking, bored, as if in an afterlife,

>and *not* waiting for
>a *deus ex machina*

to land like a rib-replacing insect on the ground.

As, in lieu of the now overwhelming need to suspend evil
>and *stop* the theodicean
>threshold being reached:

You, the beast here finally arrive: *to shipwreck sin?*

Yes, and to ensure then that every miniature model
>of Bethlehem
>(inside God's head)

>>includes a toy of
>>*you* approaching...

BATTLE OF THE GODS
only at times can our kind bear the full impact of gods
— *Friedrich Hölderlin*

—Upon a Martian terrain of metallic or ochre sheen
where spectators wear what seem like asbestos-suits

>> to protect themselves
>> from human sin,

we witness them: the bloodiest of intergalactic battles
between *all* deities in the universe, to decide which one

>> will be the first
>> to undo atheism...

upon a surface no astronomer or scientist could predict,
in which only those entities still *unreachable* by prayer
>> (and thus here
>> unsalvageable),

arrive now ready to slit the aorta of beasts, cardinals, priests,
>> in fact, any one
>> entity in retreat

(while *only* your own beast-face tattooed on gladiators
can keep Christ's nails in place, *and* the biblically dead

>> foetus of Adam
>> in all wombs...)

Until on the day of the *final* fight, when you, the beast,
(to end it?) you fly like a worm at astronomical speed or

like a split-second splinter of still undetectable shrapnel

        into God's heart:

in order to *start* finally the process of love's eternal delay
        (and claim victory?)
by slinging him, Christ: a now never-to-be theologized

        carcass across your
        shoulder-blades...

THE BEAST MEETS BISHOP BERKELEY
bodies are annihilated and created every moment or exist not at all during the intervals between our perception of them.
— George Berkeley

On the day when, suspended between an act of apprehension
and an apprehended thing, and searching for any empirical

trace of yourself, you scream (in corpuscular defiance) at Berkeley:
>'You will never ever
>annihilate the real me!'

having eluded already all scientific laws of matter, and become
something of
>a subatomic anomaly
>in the theory of forms.

THE BEAST MEDITATES ON HIS ORIGINS
I turn round
Like a dumb beast in a show,
Neither know what I am
Nor where I go
— W. B. Yeats

All attempts to explain my existence
founder on the following scant facts:
>no mother found...
>no ID bracelet...
>no baptismal robe...
>no baby fur locket...
>no obituary...
>(and the most unexplainable?)
>no celluloid
>reminder of my first tentative attempts to *slouch*,
in my family's
>back garden.

>Thus, on purgatorial terrains
>each day, *without* foetal skin
flapping, I resume, as horripilated as a
>planets' first messiah by sin:
>a slumbering of supercilious
>if not superfluous adoration,
>*somewhere in the sands of the desert*
>a dis-feathered cripple who, insane
>with internal walking-frame
inches every century closer to *my* maternity ward
>boarded-up in Christ's head...

So that, instead, now of dying
(to lead a cortège of God's undead)
I conclude that, from bungled start
to inconclusive end, I should *not*, despite
Yeats dream have ever come... but rather
should have reigned supreme
over a *more* BEAST-run, *more* BEAST-inviolable
domain; or on any new terrain
in which, day and night, its populations
work to sculpt free my presence from
the stone blank in their heads:

riving at bas-reliefs, statues, tombstones,
in fact at anything with a chisel,
until I, their new god finally appear to them.

THE BEAST STOPS LISTENING TO MUSIC

In every century, only the wind and desert,
and your wax cylinder phonograph to hand.
And the headphones of your Sony Walkman

> left playing a death metal
> song by Satan in the sand...

THE INFAMY OF THE BEAST

Today? or just when passing through any other century,
having god-dragged, myth-amended and faith-congealed
        yourself into notoriety,

so that Egyptian, Maya, Osirian civilizations (among others)
still believe they've seen you, in auguries, magic, statuary,

while writing unsubstantiated fables about you on papyrus...
        caging and circling
        you in their dreams,

until the worm-averting amphitheatre of mankind claps you
        back in from the sand...

if only to boo and hiss, because unable to miss this: the age-phases
        of each photogenic generation
        squandering their image on *you*.

        Likewise, the manacled prisoner,
        the criminal and those on death row

who pound and thump and stamp in the stalls of your soul,
as if mistaking the dimensions of their prison cell for a Roman arena

        steaming (temporarily?)
        with *only* your blood...

As the paparazzi and media battle for the rights to film you
rip off and rip out the horns and lungs of mammals
>   on live T.V.! while baiting
>   also, and killing polar bears,

>   if only to prevent you from

combating them: alcoholism, depression, drug addiction etc.

in this, the 21st century, where a new kind of rubberneck
>   is discovered *Youtubing* you,
>   at the edges of a jungle? volcano?

as you, you go on searching for it: the only unseen footage
>   of Yeats feeding *you* the fin
>   of a dolphin in Coole Park,
>   while dressed up as a nymph...

thus, accepting the fact that in the whole of this world, you, and
only you can disperse the mass media mob from the Earth,

you, you decide to burn it, the last troublesome photo of you moving...

>   So that when unable to be
>   historicized *or* money-bled,
>   you, you'll decide instead
>   to just wallop or waddle away...

until when in the final headline in the final newspaper on the final day,
and your death it is (falsely?) reported on,
>	forcing the last book
>	on eschatology to close.

THE NEW AWAKENING
> *He saw the strips of linen lying there, as well as*
> *the burial cloth that had been around Jesus's head.*
> *The cloth was folded up by itself, separate from the linen*
> — John, 20: 6-7

—Only a few hours before Jesus was due to
begin breathing through his new celestial gill

>> (*to de-lung and turn man*
>> *into a vapour on high*),

you, between the act of dying, death, and rebirth

(using the phalanx of the dead god's hand),

>> you scrawl your own
>> first theology in blood...

Until in Jerusalem (mistakenly?), you from
a tomb lunge up: decked out in grave linen,

>> and sucking on the one
>> biblical breath-canister

>> meant to be used by Christ.

THE BEAST REFUTES THE IMPORTANCE OF BARUCH SPINOZA

Because of Spinoza's obscene idea that
>> *you* could be inadequate,
or that *only* through modes and attributes
>> can your body be known.
And/or despite his geometrical planes
>> that give you *something*
>> across which to slouch...
you (everlastingly) refute him. And because (again) of Spinoza's
claim that 'In nature there is nothing contingent...'
>> you have no choice but
>> to inflame our philosopher's temple-veins!
>> by hiding out *somewhere*
between God's greater and lesser acts...
While the day-by-day increase of your biblical rage continues
>> to provide incontestable
proof that *his* intellectual attempts to master emotion are, at
>> best, an axiomatic hoax.
The final living things you garrotted in the desert and who
>> did *not* plead for their
>> life, DO (for you) make
something of an everlasting mockery of his philosophical
>> notion of *conatus*... those
last distracted few who were unable to survive your claw-wounds,
>> their own smashed ribs,
>> decapitation, etc.

So that despite agreeing *only* with the last line in the
Ethics which states, 'everything excellent is as difficult
    as it is rare', you, you'll
continue to *deflect* his theory of determinism with your glare...
    until your own soul's
     hair stands up on end

    and you, you escape into
    each and every universe
               where God's *not*.

COMPLAINT

      When the beast he inspects the Homo sapiens, the extraterrestrial,
      even Christ, for any atavistic trace of himself, howling out

      each century in despondency: 'Move on, doppelgängers!'
      His genealogy having long since been eroded by Yeats.

IDENTIFYING THE BEAST
A gaze blank and pitiless as the sun
— W. B. Yeats

The spectacle of you arriving in Bethlehem will not
be distinguishable from any other unbelievable event,
        such as (perhaps)

        a cherub thrashing,
        a tortoise winning,

        you in a Trojan horse?
For neither a deliberate disguising *or* morgue viewing
of your anatomy could expose you today as the beast. While not
        even a faith-abraded
        section of your torso
        hung in the display case
        in a theological museum

would help any one passer-by make the distinction between
        say the relic of a saint

        and *your* pineal gland.

        A theophanic mistake
        then, perhaps, if God
he were to cut free your foetus, using a surgeon's knife,
        from the womb-walls
        of the *wrong* divinity?

A reminder also, maybe, that for you to be even seen,
                it would require all
                of hell's sprinklers
to be turned on (simultaneously) to jet-clean
                your body of each of
                man's theoretical sins...

                On the day that the final
funereal procession of the faithful begins to
                elope into the mountains,
and the trinity, the last of the biblical amputees
                it aches now outwardly
                for *your* phantom limbs...

to leave who then left still capable of recognizing you
                in the wilderness?

blindfolded and left to roam as the last men of theology
                will be: sin-scripted
                and doleful zombies...

                Until you, the beast,
                you locate it: a tattoo of an arrow on your chest
                pointing to where God
                begins, and where *you*, STOP... but
                without any obvious

way now of ascertaining what part of you remains still
                unborn, or theological.

As if in priests' minds
you were still (today?) striding on hobnailed hooves
(in place of the Nazis?)
towards them...While
atheists, superstitiously,
they wait for you, for the church-closing discrepancy
of your *slouch*...For
your encroachment, age-encumbered, yet balletically
true,

when compared to the ungainly, idiotic, and supercilious
parade of man's fast
march to the grave.

THE LOOPHOLE
The ceremony of innocence is drowned
   — W. B. Yeats

Twenty-four hours before Christ's birth
we locate her, Mary, in secret burying it:

a beast made from papier-mâché and wire
(one mile north of the town of Bethlehem),

a beast which, for aeons, will remain God's
only loophole, in the event of his own death.

THE BEDOUIN

*...and in hatred turn
from every thought of God mankind has had*
— W. B. Yeats

Now *and* forever? No sandstorm will put an end
        to it: the virulence

        of his hate-prolonging
        refrain on this terrain,

        until his eschatological

visions of hyenas hunting in packs for Christ's

        lost corpse, *stop*...

and he (today?), in this desert, he gets ready

        finally to refute his own
        deity to experience it:

the *unpardonable* bliss of shepherding your

        beast soul through sin...

THE COSMOLOGICAL BEAST

Each day searching for your lost kin
in the remotest regions of deep space,
to find what only your logbook lists:
>a beast half-faded on a tablet in sand,
>>a beast ill with love on intravenous drip,
>a beast half-strangled by Judas's umbilical,
>>a beast in a pouch in God's midriff, and laughing,
>>a beast unable to reach the last peninsula of sin,
and (the most surprising?)
>>a beast argued stillborn by Aquinas' first theological feud,
these and (perhaps, less believable)
>>a beast sucking on a canister of man's last breath
(cryogenically stored
>by a bored interstellar engineer?)

Thus, today, you, the *real* beast, more agglutinative bile than
>abhorrent cosmogonic pest, you give up on the universe,
>>curse every last galaxy that has no news of you,

>bawl, snort, spit, roll yourself up

>into a knot, into the final full stop

>of the last book on cosmology…

until on the day when you (on a map?) you
>finally locate it, the planet of
>your own disincarnate birth…

a godless rock, where Yeats (you believe) still waits for you,
        (amid the unborn in a citadel)

        blindfolded, gagged, and bound...
in a city never by love to be reached, breached,

        or ever by an astronomer found.

EN ROUTE TO BETHLEHEM

The beast he makes a detour, plunges
into the Irish sea, heads for the base

of Ben Bulben, where one religion later,
we catch up with him, slumped

        against the gravestone of Yeats—
        horrified to be left alone...

SINCE THE DEATH OF YEATS

    You have been wandering
    off course, untraced and Ark-less,
somewhere in Africa,
      feigning Being, in the ebbtide
      between predestination and time...
and with only the sun's struck cymbal
      crashing inside of your brain
      as your guide...
you, heavy-lidded, you move on, day after day,
      imagining

    already ahead of you
     (in anticipation of your arrival)
    the telescopes and binoculars
poised and set up in Bethlehem, from every
window-ledge, bell tower, church...
      you abyss-drag the same unending plane,
      (stop-watched by eternity)
      while freeze-framed by a forever circling
      vulture,
          hyena, orangutang.

    —For there is nothing on
    earth now to console you, time itself
is reversed by your diasporic path,
while even
      villages close up are, to you,
      already far-off, burnt-out and smoking...

      man grows ill just to think
of you
      —And because you are too old
      and
      too young to exist in any
      one single era,
any living creature that meets the clock-lapsed
circle of your eye
      will (today?) instantaneously die, decay,
      become extinct...
      nothing can survive your survival.
      Or wear it,
your
      face, a dimension-adjustable
      mask.

—Yet some days when bored, inactive and
in search
      of a language, *any* language,
      you attempt to speak him, Yeats!
      but swallow only your own
tongue, choke
      nearly to death on his umbilical.
      As gravity, too heavy, it throws
now clods of unusable reality in your path,
      while you, sidestepping them,
you think now
      only of your own flesh left
      unwrinkled by the eternities
in Yeats' head...

    You, replacing determinism
        with your *own* choice now to plough forward,
for amid the theomachy of religious
        battles, wars, conflicts etc.

you have seen off the *Übermensch*,
        the ancient and Roman gods,
        have gang-planked the saved
out of heaven.
        You who with one single stare
        have bulldozed whole civilizations
to the ground.
        —But to deceive God again
        in yet another new century?

        well, you will need first
        to seek out a suitable alibi,
before, in haste,
        (but without embitterment)
        you kidnap and entrap a priest,
        ventriloquizing his jawbone
back to lies...

—So, as on every other day then
        (but for the last time)
        you, you'll retrieve it:
the still smoking cone of a gyre,
and place it (a shell) up to your own
ear to
        hear (as always) only the

      soul-summoning cry of Christ,
      the last lung rustle of man...

   —Until then when finally
     alone at night in the desert
and clawing up at the moon:
      where abandoned now by your
own creator,
         and feeling still 'incomplete'
         you, you give up on him, Yeats, drag
         back your head and laugh,
regurgitate finally
         his phlegm-sodden drafts...

THE EXISTENTIAL CRISIS OF THE BEAST
Everything considered, a determined soul will always manage
— Kierkegaard

On the day when feeling the void open
(like a lift shaft with no floors in thought)
and fearing suddenly that it might
start to abort beast-kind,
Bethlehem, your own gyre,
the *space-time continuum*?

we watch you beginning to propel
old fridges, worn-out tyres,
tanks, every last book in Einstein's library,
in fact, anything
that might start filling in this gaping godless
chasm opening up

now inside
of you...

(the bottomlessness suddenly of your every thought:
a vault of wall-to-wall portraits of you wearing a wig
and mask of Kierkegaard, Sartre, Beauvoir, Camus)

as, both consumed by, and dragged to, your arena-filling death
you, you lunge now violently

to one side to evade
the cold steel railings
that surround the void...
its collapsing central

crater of tubes, teeth and tentacles trying to hoover you in...

      (to begin the synchronization of church clocks
      and the fake theological countdown of eternity)

          -until, when (briefly?) the
          truth behind $E=mc2$ expires,

the universe falls through, to leave you like Sisyphus
    to shoulder the weight of God's skull...that final meaningless
        memento of the zeptosecond when you, you *almost*

          succumbed to it:
          the now never to

          be needed subplot
          of bestial anxiety,
          and Christian sin...

AFTER READING KANT'S *CRITIQUE OF PURE REASON*
   For Michael Lee Rattigan

We locate you, infuriated to be wondering why Kant's
'thing-in-itself' has been left now abandoned like God's

       lost luggage in your soul,
       or why because *you* feel
       so incapable of escaping
them: the mazes and mines of Kant's mind
        (his trapdoors in morality),

you lollop and grope about now so blindly
for a handrail in your consciousness; you, keeping alive
       what survives of your body
by feeding on the thought-rotted remains of
       the brains of the noumena...

Until you, a threshing machine of rage, you start clawing
       off the veil of 'appearance'

from each and any object in the desert that still
deceives you: a rock, a dung beetle, a dead camel...

       (while defecating the *impure*
       empirical excreta of man's soul).

Thus, finally, despite Kant's lobotomizing philosophy,
and his disembowelling dictum 'that the world cannot

    be known independent of
    any possible perception of it',
    you, unshakable, you refuse
    still point-blank to admit

that Bethlehem, at best? might *only* be a transcendental city,
    never-to-be knowingly reached.

THE LAST STAND
and they also worshipped the beast and asked,
'who is like the beast? who can make war against him?'
— Revelation 13

—The trinity wielding Adam's lost rib as a weapon
and refusing to give up on their *first* race, as, in this,

        the final merciless
        battle for mankind

(between extraditing Eve from Eden and weaning Satan off sin)
        you, the beast, survive...
        by tooth picking free

the last rotting entrails of angels from between your molars,
and by faith-quickening the final pupation period of religion
        (from God into
        Christ into you)

before the resurrection, and by finally wormhole ejecting all biblical characters
        to *another* galaxy,
        and a different role.

Until only the left-over limbs of theology can be seen here
now protruding (mutilated and charred to their fingertips),

        from the still burning
        cockpit of your soul...

THE BEAST PONDERS THE MOON LANDING

America? no, it should never have sent
those three plugged-in and quilted men
         to the stars
(too many of them on earth had already
telescoped the universe into a pinhead
of their own insignificance in deep space);
it should have rocket-launched ME
from the desert (*after* them) into the clouds,
         yes, me, who on
arrival up there on the moon would have
made a mould of it: my *first* paw-print, before
garrotting and ventriloquizing Armstrong,
forcing him to say: 'one small *slouch* for beasts,
         one giant lunge
         for beast-kind...'

For only a meteor-saddling haruspex like me can
free the universe from every scientist's map of it,
towrope galaxies, and/or stretch it, space, like a balaclava
         over and across
         Einstein's skull...
for *only* me, yes (beyond the papier-mâché
scenery that conspiracists believe constitutes
         a *fake* lunar home
         inside man's head)
was supposed to have been sent flying: a
sun-blackening satellite to orbit the earth;
         only me,

(aghast at the possibility of man achieving anything!)
by also getting there, would have lampooned
his first derisible attempt to arrive weightless
> in a non-religious place...
> *only* me
lifting up finally my visor on the moon could have revealed
> God's face.

THE LAST DAYS OF THEOLOGY
surely the second coming is at hand
  — W. B. Yeats

The beast (the utmost cause of God's goose-pimples)
is still labouring, moving slow, Zimmer frame slow,

as if dragging in tow the heavy body bag of Christ...
en route to its final destination, *en route* to a love-squandering

city whose inhabitants have almost definitely died:
pestered to extinction by the wrong god's maleficence.

A MATHEMATICAL FABLE
For James Byrne

On the last hour of the last day of every century,
    the beast he would encounter it: a number that sought,
        above all else, to eradicate him...

    a number that, to prevent the beast being born,
    refused one day to divide, multiply, or even

        subtract itself... *unless* it resulted
        in the beast being destroyed.

So, to understand why this was the case, the beast (decided) he

        had only one option open to him:

    to begin counting
        down this number
            until it was nothing...

until it returned to dust, to the last incalculable dust-
    grain of all the galaxies, until not even a whole
        race of zeros would be capable of re-hatching it.

Thus, went on the fable of the beast and the number...

until on the day when the beast (finally) he trained himself
    in mathematics, and so began to subtract this number from *himself*,
        until there was no equation left that could

       a) include this number, or
       b) result in *it*.

Thus, the beast, feeling victorious, from this day on,
    (and for all eternity) continued to rub out all trace of this
        number on blackboards, brick walls, sand etc....

    until the number could no longer divide, multiply, or
    ever again add itself to any piece of matter in the universe,

        nor to any surface
        across which the beast still slouched....

THE METAMORPHOSIS
> *And those who say 'There was when he was not'...*
> *The Catholic and Apostolic church anathematizes.*
> — Extract from the Nicene Creed (325 AD)

—When no discernible hologram inside
    God's mind resembles you, you (with chains)
        you restrain every last inhabitant on earth,

to protect them from their urges and desires for *your* flesh,
so that when you beget omnipotence, howling creeds,
(at least) three members of the council of Nicaea *believe*

        and/or begin fasting, to
        (half-doctrinally) pledge:

'your sweat is our scripture, your turbidity our goal'

        until you, in a bulldozer, crash
        through the gates of their soul...

to rush you through to the pupal stage of religion:
    from Islamist into Hinduist into Christian into *you,*
        to leave Christ's own celestial sheath abandoned....

And the saved, satiated by *your* new religion, to
begin now crawling, walking, running to meet you...

        while all priests,
        in pulpits, weep.

AN ARRIVAL
　　Surely some revelation is at hand
　　　— W. B. Yeats

The atheist, in a lab, hastily perfecting his vaccine
against a new world-variant of the *faith*-virus,

as, along corridors, in hospital, between the legs
of each cataleptic nurse, you, the beast, encroach,

dragging behind yourself a caricature of the rank
　　　　　still putrefying flesh of the
　　　　　unresurrectable on wheels...

while the Trinity, three lithe acrobats, in a waiting
　　　　　room, they spiral and unspiral

　　　　　　　(mistakenly?) the pole
　　　　　　　of Satan's charred spine.

THE INVALIDS OF ESCHATOLOGY
so dead beyond our death
— W. B. Yeats

A paramedic fighting to save Christ dying
of sin, who then himself starts killing him

(*to beach suddenly the trinity, a termite
on the first planet further than theology*)

as soteriologists, in despair, try the pope
on the phone, and the beast, in a wheelchair,

>is pushed (half-heartedly)
>home.

THE BEAST REFLECTS ON WHAT PART HIS ANATOMY HAS PLAYED IN CHRISTIANITY

        My forehead? *too* protruding,
        you could say bulging, due to all
of man's still unresolvable theological arguments.
        Yes, but so what age am I?
        Some say at least, one or two

        thousand years old, or more?

I say, ageless… if viewing myself *sub specie aeternitatis*;
as I, century after century, I've dreamt of discovering it:

        the microfilm of a truth so
        profound it might well, in
God's mind, tear down the matchstick model of his universe.
        I, with legs tottering, trying
each epoch to regurgitate the drafts of any one document that,
        if read, might possibly have

        stopped genocides, invasions,
        fake cults, religious wars etc.…

        might above all have stopped
        evil hatching in the human heart,
that which caused God (in a panic?) to crash-test dummies in the void,
        until deciding on him, *Christ*.
        Prompting me, a guard dog,

        to crouch down by his tomb

    and wait, until religion ends...

Reminding me of my mnemonic trait of forcing men
to remember only those events *my* memory forgets,

    which is why still (today?)
I feel still something of the damage done by theology
    to my frontal lobe, affecting
    (as it does) my ability to differentiate between
    the saved and the damned

(who, for me, are the *same* biologically deficient
torsos of theodicy attenuated and hooded by hate).

    Which leaves? just *this* gait,
and the imbalance of its symmetry half-eaten by the worms
    of a fake eschatological will:
    as if only a third of my torso
    was believed in by the papacy ...

trapping the trinity like a three-legged insect inside the
    cardboard box of my ear

    (every time that faith dies).

    So that, out of fear, on one,
    two, (sometimes) three legs, occasionally four
I advance, a turbine for regenerating sand
    that cancels bird flight, clogs up an angel's windpipe and
    (on a cyclical basis) blasts

back Christology to the bone...

As I, head-swivelling, I stall,
until all beasts on earth rise
up suddenly from on all fours

and, towards
           me, Jesus Christ he crawls...

SHORT SOLILOQUY OF THE POPE, BETHLEHEM

'Yeats' beast? Yeats' beast?
No, never! It will never arrive!'

resumes the pope, in old age,
atop his high rusted look-out

        among the trees.

THE BEAST BATTLES AMNESIA
a true theory of memory refutes materialism
— Henri Bergson

By wearing a sandwich board with your just birthed body painted
                 onto it... to remind
                 yourself of yourself!

and to stop reality feeling like a 'veridical hallucination'
                 (a dial turned to *nothingness*
                 inside your own head...)

as you, a turnstile, you begin letting in *only*
        those unageing dummy-torsos that resemble you, to leave
                who then holding a ticket-stub on the other side of sin?

while involuntarily shrugging each day because
                unable to remember him: *God*;

as you, (with Christ's hair plastered onto your scalp)
              you surge up dripping from the depths of man's soul...
                but unable still to dredge it, your own weight,

                    forcing you (momentarily?)
                    to negate materialism...

long enough at least for you to start searching heaven for any
          one entity there who might, possibly, recognize you?
              flushing the saved out in the process through

                    memory's porthole...

to shipwreck you in your brain, but still unable to explain:
    the neocortex, the amygdala, the hippocampus? plunging you away
        backwards from all phenomena like a gymnast into the dark!

Until, when finally, all finite beings in the universe
    (at the same time) start to remember you, you and *only*
        you…a brand-new deity *in situ*

        the first god not to be
        obliterated by thought.

THE BEAST'S CRUCIFIXION
Deformed beyond deformity, unformed,
Insipid as the dough before it is baked,
They change their bodies at a word
— *W. B. Yeats*

Between two thieves, we re-join you,
strung-up, but cackling, imagining

the sky-diving wind-rippling effect

of the resurrection upon *your* skin...

while dice-throwing heaven, the earth,
indeed, the entire universe into your

own card game of theology and sin
—taking money off the soldiers, the

chief priests, and Mary Magdalene...

until a black bibleless nothingness
moves back in, and you, in place of

Jesus, you rot back into his shrouds...

THE ARCHITECT

The day arrives when you, the beast, you assert
your right to be the biological, anatomical, theological and
> cosmological architect
> of the entire universe.
Thus, you begin to redesign, reorder and re-quantify all of
> the still extant truths
> of human cognition:
yes, but how exactly? And by what means? Well, by first
> conceiving of a hose big
> enough to put out hell,
and by repostulating the gap between good and evil
by mathematically stretching the intestines of Satan
> until *all* equations snap,
by refuting God's first egomaniacal cry 'Let there be light!'
by swallowing heaven's only lightbulb, and biting down hard
> upon its filament, until
all the planets re-blacken, and the stars go out...
> by replacing the resurrection
> of Christ with a hologram
of yourself lunging up out of every human and animal grave,
until the bush, unable to produce God's voice, it
is then doused, black-sacked and finally buried
> in man's imagination,
> forcing consciousness itself to stop, and
> no thinking thing now
able to move
> upon a single surface
> or featureless waste...

Until the day when you, untraced but relenting, you light
        up a torch to *show* God,
blind and still inarticulate with sin, a way out again
        of your own black skull.

AFTER THE UNIVERSE

All about you, no stars, only the frozen
tapestry of the confession-booth of the
            last known space,

and a light-cord dangling above your head,
            to switch on and
            off God's face.

EPILOGUE
The falcon cannot hear the falconer
— *W. B. Yeats*

Having successfully intercepted man's last prayers
to God, you, you arrive, pockmarked with the welts

        of a world's worn words:
        as, in these, the final divine

arithmetic of our days, in which falconers need
now holy hearing aids to hear their *own* birds, you

        (the animalistic patron saint
        of the theologically impaired),

you sandwich-board scripts for the religiously bewitched,

        forcing the unredeemable
        to be reduced now to extras

upon the film-set of a movie in which *no* Homo sapiens can die...
until the falcon, unrecognizable even to ornithologists,

        (in the very last scene?)

        it swoops in finally to
        land on the *wrong* wrist.

ACKNOWLEDGEMENTS

Firstly, I thank W. B. Yeats for writing 'The Second Coming', without which they would be no book.

Secondly, I thank the following friends and writers who have supported and shown an interest in the writing of this book: Rosa Richardson, Nicolas Cavaillès, Alice Oswald, Peter Oswald, James Byrne, Aaron Kent, David Spittle, Alex Pearce, Anthony Seidman, Siemon Scamell-Katz, Satsuki, Frédéric Moulin, Mark Wilson, Michèle Duclos, Martine Konorski, Tom Bland, Stephen Romer, Will Stone, and Hugh Rayment-Pickard.

Thirdly, a special mention to Michael Lee Rattigan for the cosmological and philosophical dialogues about, and re-readings of, these poems.

And fourthly, and by far the most important of all, I thank my wife Blandine Longre for her belief and tireless patience and editorial help with this book.

Also, the editors of the following magazines in which some of these poems first appeared: *The Shop, The Wolf, Poetry Salzburg, Poésie Première, Nunc, Les Carnets d'Eucharis*.

The images accompanying the poems are taken from *The History of Four-Footed Beasts and Serpents* (first published in 1607) by Edward Topsell.

LAY OUT YOUR UNREST

www.ingramcontent.com/pod-product-compliance
Lightning Source LLC
Chambersburg PA
CBHW032231080426
42735CB00008B/811